MARC REXUS

Empowered: A Guide to Financial Freedom for Adult Women

First edition

This book was professionally typeset on Reedsy.
Find out more at reedsy.com

Contents

1   Chapter 1: Introduction: The Importance of Financial...   1

2   Chapter 2: The Gender Wage Gap: Understanding and Overcoming...   3

3   Chapter 3: Financial Milestones: Setting Goals for a Secure...   5

4   Chapter 4: Saving for Success: Building an Emergency Fund...   7

5   Chapter 5: Budgeting Basics: Crafting a Personalized...   9

6   Chapter 6: Debt Management: Strategies for Paying Off Loans...   11

7   Chapter 7: Investing in Your Future: A Beginner's Guide to...   13

8   Chapter 8: Women and Retirement: Planning for a Comfortable...   16

9   Chapter 9: Real Estate: Buying, Renting, and Investing in...   18

10   Chapter 10: Insurance Matters: Protecting Yourself and Your...   20

11   Chapter 11: Tax Planning: Understanding and Maximizing...   22

12   Chapter 12: Entrepreneurship: Starting and Scaling a...   24

13   Chapter 13: Navigating the Workplace: Negotiating Raises and...   27

14   Chapter 14: Balancing Work and Family: Financial Tips for...   29

15   Chapter 15: Marriage and Money: Merging Finances and Setting...   31

16   Chapter 16: Divorce and Finances: Safeguarding Your...   33

17   Chapter 17: Estate Planning: Ensuring Your Legacy and...   35

18   Chapter 18: Financial Education: Teaching the Next...   37

19   Chapter 19: Overcoming Financial Challenges: Strategies for...   39

20   Conclusion: The Path to Financial Empowerment and...   41

1

Chapter 1: Introduction: The Importance of Financial Empowerment for Women

In today's increasingly complex world, financial literacy and empowerment are more important than ever. For women, financial empowerment isn't just about independence and security, it's also about freedom - the freedom to make choices, to take risks, to face challenges head-on, and to shape one's own destiny.

However, despite the strides women have made in various fields, many still face significant challenges when it comes to achieving financial independence. These hurdles can be attributed to a variety of factors, such as persistent wage inequality, societal norms that impact career progression, financial literacy gaps, and other gender-based disparities.

Women often carry the burden of unpaid labor, such as child-rearing and caregiving for family members, which can disrupt their career progression and long-term earning potential. Furthermore, women tend to live longer than men, increasing the need for adequate retirement savings.

Additionally, financial norms and expectations often leave women at a disadvantage. For instance, women are less likely to negotiate for higher salaries or promotions, partly due to societal norms and expectations. This behavior can result in significant lifetime income differences compared to their male counterparts.

This is where financial empowerment comes into play. Financial empowerment, at its core, is about taking control of one's financial life. It's about understanding how money works, making informed decisions, and using money as a tool to achieve one's goals and aspirations. It's about breaking down the barriers that hold women back and giving them the confidence to make their own financial decisions.

Financial empowerment doesn't happen overnight. It requires education, practice, and perseverance. It requires understanding the unique financial challenges that women face and equipping oneself with the knowledge and tools to overcome these challenges.

"Empowered: A Guide to Financial Freedom for Adult Women" is a roadmap to this journey. This book aims to equip women with the necessary knowledge and tools to take control of their financial lives. It covers a range of topics from budgeting to investing, retirement planning, and more. It provides practical strategies, tips, and real-life examples to help women navigate the often confusing world of personal finance.

By the end of this book, you will have the knowledge and confidence to make informed financial decisions, build wealth, and achieve financial independence. This book is not just about financial success, but also about empowering you to lead a life of freedom, independence, and security. It's about empowering you to become the best version of yourself.

So, let's embark on this journey towards financial empowerment together. Because every woman deserves a secure and financially independent future. Because every woman deserves to be empowered.

2

Chapter 2: The Gender Wage Gap: Understanding and Overcoming Financial Inequality

T he gender wage gap is a critical aspect of financial inequality that affects women worldwide. Despite progress and increased awareness, this gap persists, indicating a disparity between the earnings of men and women. Understanding this issue is the first step towards devising strategies to overcome it and achieve financial equality.

The gender wage gap is the average difference in pay between men and women. Often expressed as a percentage, it shows how much women earn for every dollar a man makes. According to data from the United States Census Bureau in 2020, women earned, on average, $0.82 for every dollar earned by men. This disparity is more pronounced for women of color.

Several factors contribute to the wage gap. Discrimination in hiring, pay, and promotion decisions can directly affect women's earnings. However, structural issues also play a significant role. For example, women are more likely to work part-time or take time off work due to childcare or other family responsibilities. These factors can disrupt career progression and limit earning potential. Additionally, women tend to be underrepresented in high-paying industries and overrepresented in lower-wage occupations, a phenomenon known as occupational segregation.

It's crucial to understand that the gender wage gap is not just a women's issue; it's a societal issue. It affects families, economies, and societies. When women earn less, it means less income for families, less spending in the economy, and slower economic growth.

So, how do we overcome this financial inequality? The solution lies in both systemic changes and individual actions.

Systemically, policies need to be implemented and enforced to ensure equal pay for equal work. Employers should conduct regular pay audits to identify and rectify wage disparities. Promoting transparency in pay structures can also help to combat wage discrimination. In addition, policies supporting affordable childcare, paid parental leave, and flexible work arrangements can help reduce the burden of unpaid care work and facilitate women's participation in the labor market.

On an individual level, women can equip themselves with negotiation skills to advocate for better pay and opportunities. It's also important for women to seek out mentorship and sponsorship within their industries, as these relationships can provide critical guidance and opportunities for advancement. Further, pursuing education and skills training in higher-paying fields can help to overcome occupational segregation.

Understanding the wage gap and the forces driving it is the first step to bridging it. By working together and advocating for change, we can strive towards a world where your gender does not determine your earning potential. By overcoming this financial inequality, we enable every woman to achieve her full financial potential.

3

Chapter 3: Financial Milestones: Setting Goals for a Secure Future

F inancial planning is a continuous journey, marked by key milestones that signify progress towards a secure future. Recognizing and preparing for these milestones can empower you to take charge of your financial destiny.

1. **Establishing a Budget**: The first financial milestone in any adult's life is creating and maintaining a budget. This simple yet powerful tool can help you understand your income and expenses, making it easier to plan for savings, manage debts, and allocate funds for necessities and leisure.

2. **Building an Emergency Fund**: Financial stability begins with establishing an emergency fund, a savings account designed to cover unexpected expenses or income loss. A good rule of thumb is to have at least three to six months' worth of living expenses saved.

3. **Paying off High-Interest Debt**: High-interest debts, such as credit card balances, can impede financial progress. Prioritize paying off these debts to avoid long-term financial strain and to improve your credit score.

4. **Saving for Retirement**: It's never too early to start saving for retirement. Contributing to a 401(k) or an individual retirement account (IRA) provides you with a sense of financial security and the opportunity to

grow your wealth over time.

5. **Purchasing a Home**: For many, buying a home is a significant financial milestone. This decision should be guided by thorough research, understanding of the real estate market, and consideration of your long-term financial goals.

6. **Investing in the Stock Market**: Investing is a powerful way to grow your wealth over the long term. Diversifying your investments across different types of assets can reduce risk and potentially increase returns.

7. **Starting a Business**: If entrepreneurship is in your plans, saving for startup costs and understanding business finances is crucial. This step involves a higher risk but can be rewarding both financially and personally.

8. **Planning for Children's Education**: If you plan to have children, consider starting a college fund early. This can help ease the future financial burden of tuition and other educational costs.

9. **Estate Planning**: As we grow older, it becomes increasingly important to think about estate planning. This can include drafting a will, naming beneficiaries for your assets, and considering life insurance.

10. **Achieving Financial Independence**: This ultimate milestone signifies the ability to sustain your lifestyle without having to work. Achieving this requires disciplined saving, investing, and careful financial management over many years.

Remember, everyone's financial journey is unique, and these milestones may occur at different times for different people. Additionally, your financial goals might change over time, and that's okay. What matters is regular review and adjustment of your financial plans to align with your changing needs and aspirations.

The journey towards financial security can seem overwhelming, but remember that every small step counts. With discipline, patience, and resilience, you can achieve your financial milestones and secure a prosperous future. The power to shape your financial destiny lies in your hands.

4

Chapter 4: Saving for Success: Building an Emergency Fund and Long-Term Savings

S aving is the cornerstone of financial stability. It provides a safety net for unforeseen circumstances, helps to achieve financial goals, and gives one the freedom to make choices. There are two key components to a successful saving strategy: building an emergency fund and planning for long-term savings.

Building an Emergency Fund

An emergency fund is a stash of money set aside to cover the financial surprises life throws your way. These unexpected events can be stressful and costly, such as losing a job, a sudden health issue, or major unplanned home or car repairs.

As a general rule, your emergency fund should cover three to six months of living expenses. This gives you enough buffer to weather a financial storm without having to rely on credit or loans. Remember, the goal of this fund is not to grow wealth but to provide a safety net.

To build an emergency fund:

1. Determine your monthly expenses: Include everything from housing and food costs to utilities, transportation, and personal expenses.
2. Multiply this number by three (or six, depending on your comfort level)

to get your emergency fund goal.

3. Start small if you need to and aim to set aside a certain amount from each paycheck until you reach your goal.

4. Keep your emergency fund in a separate, easily accessible account to avoid temptation but ensure quick access when needed.

Planning for Long-Term Savings

Long-term savings are meant for future financial goals, such as buying a house, starting a business, or retiring comfortably. Unlike an emergency fund, the goal of long-term savings is not just to preserve wealth but to grow it.

Here's how to effectively plan for long-term savings:

1. Set clear, specific financial goals: Whether it's a down payment for a home, college tuition, or a dream vacation, having a clear goal will motivate you to save.

2. Determine the amount needed and a timeline for each goal.

3. Consider opening separate savings accounts for each goal. This will prevent you from spending the money on other things.

4. Automate your savings: Set up automatic transfers from your checking account to your savings account. This 'set it and forget it' method ensures consistent saving.

5. Invest for growth: Consider investing a portion of your long-term savings in assets such as stocks or bonds, which have the potential to grow your money over time. Be sure to understand the risks involved and consider seeking advice from a financial advisor.

Building a solid saving strategy takes time and discipline, but the peace of mind and financial freedom it provides are worth the effort. By mastering the art of saving, you empower yourself to face any financial challenge head-on and create the future you desire.

5

Chapter 5: Budgeting Basics: Crafting a Personalized Financial Plan

A budget is an essential tool in financial planning. It allows you to understand where your money is going, manage your cash flow effectively, and stay focused on your financial goals. Here's a step-by-step guide on crafting a personalized financial plan through budgeting.

1. **Identify Your Income**: The first step in budgeting is to understand your total income. This includes your regular salary or wages, any side income, rental income, dividends, and any other sources. It's essential to use your net income (the amount you take home after taxes and other deductions) for this step.

2. **List Your Expenses**: Next, track all your expenses. Start with fixed expenses, which are the same each month, such as rent or mortgage payments, car payments, and insurance premiums. Then, move to variable expenses, which fluctuate month to month. These include groceries, utility bills, transportation costs, and entertainment expenses. Remember to also include periodic expenses, such as annual insurance premiums or car maintenance costs.

3. **Set Financial Goals**: Whether it's saving for a down payment, paying off debt, or saving for retirement, having financial goals gives purpose

to your budget. Separate your goals into short-term (within a year), mid-term (1–5 years), and long-term (5+ years) to help prioritize.

4. **Create Your Budget**: There are several budgeting methods, and the key is finding what works best for you. A common method is the 50/30/20 rule, where 50% of your income goes towards necessities (rent, utilities, groceries), 30% towards discretionary spending (dining out, hobbies), and 20% towards savings and debt repayment.

5. **Track Your Spending**: Regularly tracking your spending against your budget is crucial. This helps you stay on track and make adjustments as necessary. There are several apps and tools available to help with this, or you can use a simple spreadsheet.

6. **Adjust as Necessary**: Life is unpredictable, and your budget should be flexible enough to accommodate changes. Regularly review your budget, at least monthly, and make adjustments as necessary. It's okay if your budget isn't perfect from the start; the key is to start and adjust along the way.

Remember, the purpose of a budget isn't to restrict your spending but to empower you to make informed decisions with your money. It's a tool to help you achieve your financial goals and provide a sense of control over your financial future.

Budgeting is a habit, and like any habit, it takes time to develop. Start today, be patient with yourself, and remember: every step, no matter how small, brings you closer to your financial goals.

6

Chapter 6: Debt Management: Strategies for Paying Off Loans and Credit Cards

D ebt, whether from student loans, credit cards, or a mortgage, is a reality for many. While having debt can be a normal part of one's financial life, uncontrolled debt can become a burden. However, with the right strategies, you can manage your debt effectively and work towards a debt-free life.

Understanding Your Debt

The first step in managing debt is to understand what you owe. List all your debts, including the creditor, total amount of the debt, monthly payment, and interest rate. This overview will give you a clear understanding of your debt situation.

Budgeting for Debt Repayment

Include debt payments in your budget. It's important to make at least the minimum payment on all your debts each month to avoid penalties and damage to your credit score.

Debt Repayment Strategies

There are two popular strategies for paying off multiple debts:

1. **Debt Snowball Method**: This strategy involves paying off debts in order of smallest to largest balance, regardless of interest rate. The idea is

that paying off smaller debts first will create a psychological boost and momentum to keep going.

2. **Debt Avalanche Method**: Here, you pay off debts in order of highest to lowest interest rate. This strategy saves more money in interest over time but may take longer to see results compared to the debt snowball method.

Choose a method that suits your financial situation and motivates you the most.

Prioritize High-Interest Debt

High-interest debt (often credit cards) can grow rapidly and consume a significant portion of your income. Prioritizing these debts can save you money in the long run.

Consider Debt Consolidation

If you have multiple high-interest debts, debt consolidation may be a good option. This strategy involves taking out a new loan to pay off your existing debts, leaving you with one monthly payment, often at a lower interest rate. Be cautious, though, as this method requires discipline to avoid accumulating new debt.

Seek Professional Help

If you feel overwhelmed by debt, don't hesitate to seek help from a credit counselor or financial advisor. They can provide advice tailored to your situation and even negotiate with creditors on your behalf.

Practice Good Financial Habits

Preventing future debt is just as important as paying off current debt. This includes sticking to a budget, building an emergency fund, and using credit wisely.

Remember, becoming debt-free won't happen overnight, but with discipline, determination, and the right strategies, you can manage your debt effectively and work towards financial freedom. The path to a debt-free life begins with a single step, so start your journey today.

7

Chapter 7: Investing in Your Future: A Beginner's Guide to the Stock Market

I nvesting in the stock market is a powerful way to grow your wealth and secure your financial future. However, for beginners, the world of stocks can seem daunting. Here's a beginner-friendly guide to help you understand and navigate the stock market.

Understanding the Basics

The stock market is where buyers and sellers trade shares of publicly traded companies. When you buy a share of stock, you essentially own a small piece of that company and become a shareholder.

Investing in stocks can generate profits in two ways: through the appreciation of the stock price over time, and through dividends, which are a portion of the company's earnings distributed to shareholders.

Setting Financial Goals

Before diving into stock investing, it's essential to establish your financial goals. Are you saving for retirement, a down payment on a house, or your child's college tuition? Your financial goals, along with your risk tolerance and investment timeline, will guide your investment strategy.

Starting with a Diversified Portfolio

Diversification involves spreading your investments across various types of assets to reduce risk. Instead of buying shares from just one company, you should aim to build a diversified portfolio consisting of shares from multiple companies across different sectors. This way, if one investment performs poorly, others might perform well and balance out your losses.

For beginners, mutual funds and exchange-traded funds (ETFs) are a great way to achieve diversification. These funds pool money from many investors to buy a broad range of stocks, bonds, or other assets.

Understanding Risk and Reward

Investing in stocks involves risk, as the market can be volatile and stock prices fluctuate. However, historically, the stock market has provided substantial returns over the long term. It's crucial to understand that higher potential returns often come with higher risk.

Long-Term Investment Strategy

One common and effective strategy for stock investing is "buy and hold," which involves buying stocks and holding onto them for a long time, regardless of market fluctuations. This approach relies on the idea that over the long term, the stock market will deliver a good rate of return despite periods of volatility.

Getting Started with a Brokerage Account

To buy stocks, you'll need to open a brokerage account. There are plenty of online brokers that offer easy-to-use platforms and low fees. Look for a broker that suits your needs and preferences.

Educating Yourself

Stay informed about financial news and understand the businesses you're investing in. Books, online courses, and financial news sources are great educational tools.

Consulting a Financial Advisor

A financial advisor can provide personalized advice based on your financial situation and goals. If you're unsure about making investment decisions on your own, consulting a professional can be beneficial.

Investing in the stock market may seem complex, but it doesn't have to be. With time, patience, and a willingness to learn, you can start growing your wealth and secure your financial future. Remember, the journey of investing is a marathon, not a sprint. Start slow, be consistent, and let your investments grow over time.

8

Chapter 8: Women and Retirement: Planning for a Comfortable and Independent Future

P lanning for retirement is crucial for everyone, but it's especially important for women. Due to factors like longer life expectancy and the gender wage gap, women may face unique challenges in retirement planning. Here's a guide to help women plan for a comfortable and independent future.

Understanding the Unique Challenges

Women tend to live longer than men, which means they'll need more retirement savings to cover their longer lifespan. Additionally, women often have lower lifetime earnings due to the gender wage gap or time taken off to care for family, which can result in lower retirement savings. Understanding these challenges can help you plan more effectively.

Start Saving Early

The earlier you start saving for retirement, the more time your money has to grow. Even small amounts can add up over time, thanks to the power of compounding interest. Make sure to take advantage of retirement accounts like a 401(k) or an individual retirement account (IRA).

Take Advantage of Employer-Sponsored Retirement Plans

If your employer offers a retirement plan, like a 401(k), take full advantage of it. If your employer matches contributions, try to contribute at least enough to get the full match—it's essentially free money.

Diversify Your Investments

Don't put all your eggs in one basket. Diversify your investments across different types of assets (stocks, bonds, real estate, etc.). This can help reduce risk and potentially increase returns.

Consider Your Social Security Benefits

Social Security benefits play a significant role in many women's retirement plans. You can start receiving benefits as early as 62, but waiting until your full retirement age (or even later, up to age 70) will increase your monthly benefit amount.

Plan for Healthcare Costs

Women typically have higher healthcare costs in retirement, partly due to longer lifespans. Consider these costs in your retirement planning and explore options for health insurance beyond Medicare.

Estate Planning

Estate planning is an essential part of retirement planning. This includes drafting a will, naming beneficiaries for your assets, and considering a healthcare proxy and power of attorney. This can ensure your wishes are carried out and can provide peace of mind for you and your loved ones.

Seek Professional Advice

A financial advisor can provide personalized advice and help you create a comprehensive retirement plan. They can consider your current financial situation, future goals, and risk tolerance to craft a plan tailored to you.

Remember, it's never too late or too early to start planning for retirement. While women may face unique challenges when it comes to retirement, with thoughtful planning and smart strategies, you can build a secure and comfortable future. Take control of your financial future today—it's one of the most empowering steps you can take.

Chapter 9: Real Estate: Buying, Renting, and Investing in Property

Real estate plays a crucial role in personal finance, from providing a home to potentially generating income and appreciating in value. This chapter will cover the basics of buying, renting, and investing in property.

Buying a Home

Purchasing a home is often the largest investment people make in their lifetime. Here are some key points to consider:

1. **Budgeting and Financing**: Determine what you can afford. Factor in the down payment, mortgage payments, property taxes, insurance, and maintenance. Shop around for a mortgage to find the best rates and terms.

2. **Location**: The location of your home can impact its value, your lifestyle, and even your daily commute. Consider proximity to schools, work, amenities, and public transport.

3. **Home Inspection**: A professional home inspection can reveal potential issues with the property. This can help you avoid expensive surprises down the line.

Renting a Property

Renting can offer flexibility and freedom from maintenance responsibilities. When renting:

1. Understand the terms of your lease agreement.
2. Be aware of your rights as a tenant, which can vary by location.
3. Consider renter's insurance to protect your belongings.

Investing in Real Estate

Real estate can be a profitable investment, providing income through rent and potential appreciation in property value. Two common ways to invest are rental properties and real estate investment trusts (REITs).

1. **Rental Properties**: This involves purchasing a property and renting it out. You'll need to manage the property or hire a property manager. Consider the potential rental income, the condition of the property, location, and your ability to manage it.
2. **Real Estate Investment Trusts (REITs)**: REITs are companies that own, operate, or finance income-producing real estate. You can invest in REITs through a brokerage account, similar to buying stocks. They offer a way to invest in real estate without having to own a physical property.

Working with Professionals

Whether you're buying, renting, or investing, working with professionals like real estate agents, mortgage brokers, and property managers can help guide you through the process.

Real estate can be a complex field, but it can also provide significant financial benefits. By understanding the basics of buying, renting, and investing in property, you can make informed decisions that align with your financial goals. Always consider your personal circumstances and, if needed, seek advice from financial and real estate professionals to assist in your real estate journey.

10

Chapter 10: Insurance Matters: Protecting Yourself and Your Loved Ones

I nsurance serves as a financial safety net, protecting you and your loved ones from unexpected losses. Different types of insurance cover different types of risks. This chapter will explain key insurance types and why they matter in your financial journey.

Health Insurance

Health insurance is vital for covering medical costs, from routine check-ups to hospital stays. Many employers offer health insurance, but you can also buy it individually. When choosing a plan, consider the premium, deductible, out-of-pocket maximum, and what services are covered.

Life Insurance

Life insurance provides financial security to your dependents in case of your death. If you have children, a spouse who depends on your income, or significant debts, life insurance is especially important. There are two main types: term life (covering a specific period) and whole life (which includes an investment component and lasts as long as you pay the premiums).

Disability Insurance

Disability insurance provides income if you're unable to work due to injury or illness. There are two types: short-term (covering a few months) and long-term (which can last until retirement age). If you rely heavily on your income, it's worthwhile to consider disability insurance.

Auto Insurance

If you own a car, auto insurance is a must. Not only is it legally required in most places, but it can also cover the costs associated with an accident. Auto insurance policies can cover liability, collision, comprehensive damage, and personal injury.

Homeowner's/Renter's Insurance

Homeowner's insurance covers your home and belongings in case of events like fires, theft, or certain natural disasters. If you have a mortgage, homeowner's insurance is typically required.

If you rent, your landlord's insurance doesn't cover your belongings. Renter's insurance can protect your personal property and may provide liability coverage.

Long-Term Care Insurance

As we age, there's a chance we may need assistance with daily living activities. Long-term care insurance can help cover the costs of this care, whether it's in-home or at a nursing facility.

Evaluating Insurance Needs

Everyone's insurance needs are different. Factors to consider include your financial situation, family status, health, and risk tolerance. As your situation changes, your insurance needs may change too.

Working with an Insurance Agent

An insurance agent can help you navigate your insurance options and tailor coverage to your needs. They can explain policy details and answer any questions you have.

Insurance is an important part of a sound financial plan. While it may feel like an unnecessary cost when times are good, it provides essential protection when things go wrong. Remember, the purpose of insurance is not to make you rich, but to prevent you from becoming poor due to unforeseen events.

11

Chapter 11: Tax Planning: Understanding and Maximizing Deductions and Credits

T ax planning plays an essential role in managing your personal finances. An understanding of how taxes work, coupled with strategic planning, can help you maximize deductions and credits, reducing your overall tax liability.

Understanding Your Tax Bracket

In the United States, the federal income tax system is progressive, which means the rate of taxation increases as the taxable amount increases. Understanding your tax bracket can help you plan for the amount of tax you'll owe and make strategic financial decisions.

Tax Deductions

Tax deductions reduce the amount of your income that's subject to tax. Here are a few common ones:

1. **Standard Deduction**: A flat dollar amount that reduces your taxable income. The amount varies depending on your filing status.
2. **Itemized Deductions**: These include certain expenses you've paid throughout the year, such as mortgage interest, state and local taxes, and charitable donations. You can claim itemized deductions instead of the standard deduction if it results in lower taxable income.

3. **Above-the-Line Deductions**: These are deductions you can take even if you choose the standard deduction. Examples include student loan interest and contributions to a traditional Individual Retirement Account (IRA).

Tax Credits

Unlike deductions, which reduce your taxable income, tax credits directly reduce your tax liability. Some common tax credits include the Child Tax Credit, Earned Income Tax Credit (EITC), and American Opportunity Tax Credit (AOTC for education expenses).

Retirement Contributions

Contributions to traditional retirement accounts like a 401(k) or IRA can be deducted from your income, lowering your tax liability. The Roth versions of these accounts are funded with after-tax money, meaning you don't get a tax deduction now, but you can withdraw the money tax-free in retirement.

Health Savings Account (HSA) and Flexible Spending Account (FSA)

Contributions to an HSA or FSA can be deducted from your income. These accounts allow you to set aside pre-tax money for eligible health care expenses.

Tax Planning Strategies

Tax planning involves strategies to minimize your tax liability. These might include timing income and deductions, choosing between itemized and standard deductions, and making the most of tax-advantaged accounts.

Professional Tax Advice

Tax laws are complex and change frequently. A tax professional or Certified Public Accountant (CPA) can provide advice tailored to your situation, help you plan strategically, and ensure you're in compliance with all tax laws.

While taxes can be complex, understanding the basics can help you make smarter financial decisions and potentially save you money. By maximizing your deductions and credits and utilizing tax-advantaged accounts, you can ensure you're not paying more tax than necessary.

12

Chapter 12: Entrepreneurship: Starting and Scaling a Successful Business

S tarting a business can be a rewarding way to take control of your financial future. However, entrepreneurship involves risks and challenges. This chapter will guide you through the process of starting and scaling a successful business.

Business Idea and Market Research

An entrepreneurial journey starts with a business idea. It could solve a problem, meet a need, or offer something new or improved. Once you have an idea, conduct market research to understand your potential customers and competition.

Business Plan

A business plan outlines what your business does, your goals, target market, competition, marketing and sales strategy, organizational structure, and financial projections. It can help you stay focused and can be crucial for securing financing.

Legal Considerations

Choose a business structure that suits your needs. Common types include sole proprietorship, partnership, limited liability company (LLC), and corporation. Each has its implications for liability, taxation, and management structure. It's also essential to understand relevant laws and regulations, including licenses and permits you may need.

Financing Your Business

There are several ways to fund your business, including self-financing, loans, investors, or crowdfunding. Each comes with its considerations, and what works best will depend on your business type and stage.

Building a Brand

Your brand is how your business is perceived. It includes your business name, logo, and how you communicate with customers. Your brand should convey what your business stands for and what sets it apart.

Marketing and Sales

A marketing strategy is crucial for attracting and retaining customers. This might involve social media marketing, email marketing, SEO, and content marketing. Sales strategies involve how you plan to sell your products or services and maintain relationships with customers.

Operations and Management

Effective operations management involves coordinating your resources to meet your business goals. This includes everything from managing inventory to hiring and training staff to customer service.

Financial Management

Keeping accurate and up-to-date financial records is crucial. This includes income, expenses, cash flow, and financial forecasts. Financial management also involves pricing your products or services profitably and managing costs.

Scaling Your Business

As your business grows, you may need to hire more employees, expand your offerings, or enter new markets. Scaling a business involves challenges, and it's crucial to plan for growth to maintain quality and customer satisfaction.

Seeking Advice and Mentoring

An experienced mentor can provide guidance, feedback, and support as you start and grow your business. Networking with other entrepreneurs can also provide valuable insights and opportunities.

Starting a business can be a challenging yet rewarding journey. It requires determination, resilience, and a willingness to learn and adapt. It's not just about achieving financial independence—it's about bringing a vision to life, creating value for others, and possibly leaving a lasting impact.

13

Chapter 13: Navigating the Workplace: Negotiating Raises and Promotions

Navigating the workplace effectively involves understanding how to advocate for yourself, especially when it comes to negotiating raises and promotions. Here's how you can approach these discussions with confidence and professionalism.

Understanding Your Worth

Before entering any negotiation, it's essential to understand your worth. Research industry norms for your role, considering factors like your level of experience, skills, and location. Websites like Glassdoor and Payscale can provide salary ranges for various positions across different industries and cities.

Track Your Accomplishments

Keep a record of your accomplishments at work. Be specific: track your completed projects, any quantitative improvements you've made, or positive feedback from colleagues or clients. These accomplishments can serve as concrete evidence of your contributions to the company.

Timing is Key

Ideally, raise and promotion discussions should occur during annual performance reviews. However, if these aren't practiced in your workplace, or if you've taken on significantly more responsibility, it may be appropriate to request a discussion at a different time.

Prepare Your Case

When you're ready to ask for a raise or promotion, prepare a clear, concise case. Highlight your achievements, responsibilities, and the market rate for your role. The goal is to demonstrate your value and justify your request.

Communicating Effectively

Request a formal meeting with your manager to discuss your compensation. During the meeting, express your enthusiasm for your role and the company before moving on to your request. Be direct, professional, and confident. Use your prepared material to back up your request.

Negotiating

If your initial request is not accepted, this is where negotiation skills come into play. You might suggest a smaller raise or a plan for a future salary increase based on defined objectives. If the budget is the issue, perhaps discuss non-monetary compensation, like more vacation time, flexible hours, or professional development opportunities.

Handling Rejection

If your request is denied, ask for feedback. It might be about budget constraints, or maybe there are areas where you need to improve. Use this as a learning opportunity and ask for specific goals to work towards before the next review.

Planning for the Future

Whether you secure the raise or promotion or not, it's important to continuously plan for your future. Regularly update your skills and knowledge, set new goals, and continue tracking your accomplishments.

Navigating the workplace and negotiating raises and promotions is not just about increasing your earning potential. It's also about recognizing your worth, advocating for yourself, and ensuring your contributions are appropriately valued. Remember, negotiation is a skill, and like any skill, it improves with practice.

14

Chapter 14: Balancing Work and Family: Financial Tips for Working Mothers

B eing a working mother is a constant balancing act, managing professional ambitions alongside the demands of raising a family. Having a solid financial plan can provide stability and security. Here are some financial tips to assist working mothers in navigating this journey.

Budgeting and Saving

A clear budget helps in managing the family's income and expenses effectively. Prioritize savings and consider automatic transfers to a savings account. Saving for an emergency fund can provide a safety net for unforeseen circumstances.

Planning for Childcare Costs

Childcare often represents a significant portion of a family's budget. Explore various options such as daycare, nannies, or family help, and consider their cost implications. Some employers offer dependent care flexible spending accounts (FSAs), which allow you to use pre-tax dollars for eligible expenses.

Investing in Education

Start saving early for your children's education. In the U.S., 529 plans offer tax advantages for education savings. Regular, small contributions can add up over time.

Insurance and Estate Planning

Ensure you have sufficient life and disability insurance to provide for your family if something happens to you. Also, consider creating a will and appointing a guardian for your children, if you haven't done so.

Retirement Planning

It's essential not to let immediate family needs overshadow your long-term retirement savings. If possible, contribute enough to your employer-sponsored retirement plan to get any available matching contributions.

Flexible Work Arrangements

Balancing work and family often involves negotiating flexibility. This might mean flexible hours, remote work, or part-time arrangements. While this could affect your income, it might save costs in other areas, like childcare.

Self-Care

Although not directly a financial tip, remember that self-care is important. Investing time in your health and well-being can ultimately help you maintain your earning potential and avoid potential health-related costs.

Financial Education for Kids

Teaching your kids about money can set them up for financial success in adulthood. Simple lessons about saving, spending wisely, and the value of money can be incorporated into everyday experiences.

Balancing work and family as a mother is challenging, but financial planning can alleviate some stresses. By making thoughtful financial decisions, working mothers can not only provide for their families but also invest in their own financial futures, ensuring long-term security and prosperity.

15

Chapter 15: Marriage and Money: Merging Finances and Setting Joint Goals

Money is a common topic of disagreement in marriages. However, with open communication, clear agreements, and shared financial goals, couples can navigate their finances successfully. Here's a guide on merging finances and setting joint financial goals in marriage.

Open Communication

Honest and open communication about money is crucial. Discuss your financial histories, current financial situation, money habits, beliefs about money, and financial goals. Regularly check in on these topics as they can change over time.

Merging Finances

Couples have different options when it comes to managing finances: merging everything, keeping everything separate, or a hybrid approach (separate accounts for personal spending and joint accounts for shared expenses). Each approach has its pros and cons, and what works best depends on your individual circumstances and preferences.

Budgeting Together

Creating a joint budget can help manage your combined income and shared expenses. It's crucial to be honest about all sources of income, debts, and recurring expenses. A joint budget can help ensure fairness, accountability, and shared financial responsibility.

Debt Management

If either of you brings debt into the marriage, discuss how you'll handle it. Will you tackle it together, or will the person who incurred the debt be responsible for paying it off? Consider seeking professional advice if dealing with significant debt.

Setting Joint Financial Goals

Discuss your short-term and long-term financial goals. These could include saving for a home, starting a family, paying off debt, or planning for retirement. Make sure your budget aligns with these goals.

Retirement Planning

Talk about your expectations for retirement and start planning for it. If both of you are working, take advantage of employer-sponsored retirement plans, especially if they offer matching contributions.

Insurance and Estate Planning

Ensure you both have appropriate insurance coverages, including health, life, and disability insurance. Update your beneficiaries on insurance policies and retirement accounts. Consider creating or updating your wills and discuss your wishes regarding medical care and power of attorney.

Financial Professional

A financial advisor can provide objective advice and help you create a financial plan that takes both your goals into account. Similarly, a tax professional can advise on the tax implications of marriage.

In a marriage, you're a team. That includes working together to make financial decisions. While it can be challenging to merge finances and set joint goals, doing so can provide financial stability and allow you to achieve shared dreams. Remember, there's no 'one size fits all' approach - the key is to find what works best for your relationship.

16

Chapter 16: Divorce and Finances: Safeguarding Your Financial Future

D ivorce is a challenging life event, and its financial implications can be significant. Understanding how to navigate these changes can help safeguard your financial future.

Understanding the Process

The divorce process varies by location, but it typically involves dividing marital property and determining spousal and child support. If you're unfamiliar with the process, consider hiring a divorce attorney to guide you through.

Gathering Financial Documentation

Collect all relevant financial documents, including bank statements, investment accounts, retirement accounts, real estate documents, tax returns, and debt records. These will provide a clear picture of your marital finances.

Assessing Assets and Debts

Understand which assets are considered marital and which are individual. This often depends on when the asset was acquired and how it was used. Similarly, understand which debts you may be responsible for.

Financial Professionals

Consider working with a financial advisor experienced in divorce. They can provide objective advice and help you understand the financial implications of your divorce settlement. A Certified Divorce Financial Analyst (CDFA) specializes in this area.

Spousal and Child Support

If you have children, you'll need to consider child support and possibly spousal support (alimony). Understand how these are calculated and what you might expect to receive or pay.

Retirement Accounts

Dividing retirement accounts can be complex and might require a Qualified Domestic Relations Order (QDRO). Penalties for early withdrawal can often be avoided in divorce, but taxes can still apply. Ensure you understand how your retirement savings will be affected.

Insurance

Make sure you have health insurance coverage. If you were covered under your spouse's employer's plan, you may need to get your own. Also, review your life and disability insurance needs.

Estate Planning

Update your will, power of attorney, and healthcare proxy. Also, update beneficiaries on your retirement accounts and insurance policies.

Rebuilding Financially

Post-divorce, you'll likely need to adjust your budget and financial plans to fit your new situation. This might involve reducing expenses, increasing income, or both. It's also a good time to rebuild emergency savings and refocus on retirement planning.

Divorce can have significant financial implications, but with the right planning and professional advice, you can navigate this challenging time and safeguard your financial future. Remember, it's important to take care of your mental and emotional health as well as your financial health during this difficult time.

17

Chapter 17: Estate Planning: Ensuring Your Legacy and Protecting Your Loved Ones

Estate planning is a process that helps you specify your wishes regarding your assets after your death. It's about ensuring your legacy, protecting your loved ones, and providing for your own care if you become unable to make decisions. Here are key elements to consider in estate planning.

Wills

A will is a legal document that outlines how you want your assets distributed after your death. It can also specify guardians for minor children. If you die without a will, state law will determine how your assets are divided, which may not align with your wishes.

Trusts

A trust is a legal entity that holds assets for the benefit of specific individuals (beneficiaries). There are various types of trusts, and they can provide benefits such as avoiding probate (the legal process to distribute assets after death), providing for minors or special needs individuals, or minimizing estate taxes.

Beneficiary Designations

Certain assets, like life insurance policies and retirement accounts, are distributed based on beneficiary designations. Ensure these are up to date and align with your overall estate plan.

Durable Power of Attorney

A durable power of attorney designates someone to manage your financial affairs if you become incapacitated. This person can handle tasks like paying bills, managing investments, or selling property.

Healthcare Power of Attorney and Living Will

A healthcare power of attorney designates someone to make healthcare decisions for you if you're unable to do so. A living will specifies your wishes for end-of-life medical care.

Estate Taxes

Understand potential estate tax liabilities. Federal estate tax only applies to larger estates, but some states also impose estate or inheritance taxes. Certain strategies, like gifting assets during your lifetime or setting up trusts, can help minimize estate taxes.

Professional Help

Estate laws are complex and vary by state, so it's often beneficial to work with a knowledgeable attorney. Financial planners and tax professionals can also provide valuable advice.

Estate planning involves considering some difficult questions, but it's a critical aspect of financial planning. It ensures your wishes are followed, protects your loved ones, and can provide peace of mind. Remember, estate planning isn't just for the wealthy - everyone can benefit from understanding how their assets will be handled after their death.

18

Chapter 18: Financial Education: Teaching the Next Generation About Money Management

F inancial education is one of the most important gifts we can give to the next generation. By teaching young people about money management, we equip them with skills that can lead to financial independence and security. Here's how to go about it.

Start Early

Introduce basic money concepts at an early age. Young children can begin to understand the concepts of earning, spending, saving, and sharing. Using a piggy bank or clear jar to save coins can help visualize the growth of savings over time.

Allowance and Earning

Consider providing an allowance to older children to help them learn budgeting firsthand. You might link the allowance to chores, teaching the correlation between work and income.

Budgeting and Saving

Help children create a simple budget, allocating money to spending, saving, and sharing. Encourage saving for larger goals, demonstrating the idea of delayed gratification.

Understanding Value

Teach kids to compare prices and understand the value of items. Take them shopping and discuss why you choose certain products over others.

Banking and Interest

Once they're old enough, help them open a savings account. Explain how interest works and the importance of saving for the future.

Credit and Debt

Teenagers should understand the basics of credit and debt, including credit cards, student loans, car loans, and mortgages. Explain the concept of interest, the importance of timely repayments, and the potential pitfalls of debt.

Investing

Introduce the concept of investing, explaining stocks, bonds, and mutual funds. Discuss the importance of diversification and the long-term nature of investing.

Influence of Advertising

Teach children to be aware of the influence of advertising and peer pressure on spending habits. Encourage them to think critically about their wants and needs.

Financial Responsibility

Discuss the concept of financial responsibility, including timely payment of bills, managing debt, and planning for unexpected expenses.

Higher Education and Career Planning

As teenagers approach adulthood, discuss the financial implications of higher education and career choices. This includes tuition costs, potential student loans, earning potential, and job market trends.

Financial education for the next generation is about more than just understanding money. It's about empowering them to make informed decisions, handle financial challenges, and build a secure financial future. Remember, the goal isn't to create financial experts but to instill a fundamental understanding of money management and its lifelong implications.

19

Chapter 19: Overcoming Financial Challenges: Strategies for Resilience and Triumph

O vercoming financial challenges is a common thread in everyone's life. It can take shape in various forms - job loss, excessive debt, health issues, or significant life changes like divorce or death of a partner. No matter the situation, resilience, determination, and strategic planning can help navigate through these financial difficulties, leading to eventual triumph. Here are key strategies to employ:

Financial Literacy

Education is the first step in overcoming financial difficulties. Understand the basics of budgeting, saving, investing, debt management, and retirement planning. Use resources like books, online courses, podcasts, and financial advisors to increase your knowledge.

Budgeting and Expense Management

Creating a budget gives you a clear picture of your income and expenses, helping you identify areas for cost reduction. Prioritize essential expenses and cut back on non-essentials.

Emergency Fund

Building an emergency fund can provide a financial cushion in times of crisis.

Aim for three to six months of living expenses.

Increasing Income

Look for ways to increase your income. This could involve negotiating a raise, finding a higher-paying job, starting a side hustle, or turning a hobby into a revenue source.

Managing Debt

High-interest debt can exacerbate financial difficulties. Develop a plan to pay down your debts, starting with the ones with the highest interest rates. Consult with a debt counselor if needed.

Insurance and Health Costs

Ensure you have adequate insurance coverage to protect against significant financial risks. For high medical costs, talk to your healthcare providers about payment plans or financial assistance programs.

Investing for the Future

Despite current financial challenges, don't overlook the future. Continue to invest for long-term goals as much as possible, especially retirement.

Seeking Professional Help

Financial planners, credit counselors, and tax professionals can provide invaluable guidance during financial hardships. They can help you create a plan and keep you accountable.

Maintaining Mental and Emotional Health

Financial stress can take a toll on your mental and emotional health. Seek support from friends, family, or professionals. Remember to take time for self-care and stress-relieving activities.

Overcoming financial difficulties often requires significant effort and discipline, but it can lead to a stronger financial future. Remember, the path to financial resilience and triumph is often not a straight line. There will be setbacks and challenges, but with perseverance and strategic action, you can navigate through financial adversities.

20

Conclusion: The Path to Financial Empowerment and Independence

T he journey to financial empowerment and independence is unique for each person, characterized by individual aspirations, challenges, and triumphs. Yet, certain principles remain universally applicable and serve as beacons guiding us on this journey.

Financial Literacy

A strong understanding of financial concepts, from budgeting to investing, is critical. This education is the foundation of all financial decisions and empowers us to navigate the financial world confidently.

Proactive Planning

Rather than reacting to financial situations as they arise, proactive planning allows us to anticipate our financial needs and challenges. This involves setting financial goals, crafting a personalized financial plan, and regularly revisiting it to make necessary adjustments.

Savings and Investments

The importance of building an emergency fund and long-term savings cannot be overstated. Likewise, investing plays a crucial role in achieving financial independence. The power of compound interest allows our money to grow over time, helping us reach our financial goals more quickly.

Debt Management

Understanding how to manage debt effectively is a key component of financial health. This involves making regular, timely payments, prioritizing high-interest debt, and avoiding unnecessary debt.

Career Advancement

Our income from work plays a substantial role in our financial journey. Therefore, advocating for ourselves in the workplace, seeking promotions and raises, and potentially pursuing additional income streams can accelerate our path to financial independence.

Life Transitions

Major life transitions like marriage, children, divorce, and retirement significantly impact our financial situation. Planning for these events can help ensure we're financially prepared when they occur.

Insurance and Estate Planning

Protecting ourselves and our loved ones from financial uncertainty through appropriate insurance coverage is crucial. Similarly, estate planning ensures that our assets are distributed according to our wishes and our loved ones are taken care of after our demise.

Financial Resilience

Building financial resilience helps us weather financial challenges and setbacks. This involves maintaining a flexible mindset, continually learning, and making strategic adjustments to our financial plan as needed.

Legacy and Financial Education

Financial empowerment is not only about our own financial independence but also about impacting future generations. Teaching the next generation about money management equips them with the tools for their own financial empowerment.

As we conclude, remember that financial empowerment and independence is not a destination, but a journey. It's a continuous process of learning, adapting, and growing. It requires patience, discipline, resilience, and often involves overcoming challenges. However, the rewards – peace of mind, freedom of choice, security, and the ability to live the life we desire – are immeasurably valuable. Your path to financial empowerment and independence starts now. Embrace it, and embark on the journey towards a financially secure future.